From These Outskirts

poems by

Claire McGoff

Finishing Line Press
Georgetown, Kentucky

From These Outskirts

ACKNOWLEDGMENTS

I would like to thank the following publications where these poems
first appeared, sometimes in different title and/or form.

Beyond Words: "Heimweh"

Innisfree Poetry Journal: "Winter Lullaby," "The Falls"

Image Magazine: "The Dawning"

Wingless Dreamer: "Emperor Penguins"

I'd like to express gratitude to my teachers, Martin Galvin, Stanley
Plumly, David Keplinger; to Maurice Manning and my other
supervisors at Warren Wilson College; to Stewart Moss; to Betty
Adcock; to my 3 writing groups; and to my husband, Chris, and my
wonderful family for all your support.

Publisher: Leah Huete de Maines
Editor: Christen Kincaid
Cover Art: Rebecca Rand
Author Photo: Chris McGoff
Cover Design: Rebecca Rand
Typeface Advisor: Michael Ponton
Typeface: Miller

Order online: www.finishinglinepress.com
also available on amazon.com

Author inquiries and mail orders:
Finishing Line Press
P. O. Box 1626
Georgetown, Kentucky 40324
U. S. A.

Table of Contents

I.

II.

For my mother,
Vesta

and for my sister,
Ruth

"The universe of poetry is the universe of emotional truth. Our material is in the way we feel and the way we remember"

Muriel Rukeyser

I.

Heimweh*

Before I knew her name was Hilda.
Before I knew her family had moved
from Germany to Russia
to Oklahoma to Texas to farm.
Before I learned it was soap
she was making—mixing lye saved
from rainwater and ash with fat,
and stirring until the liquid
slid off the paddle just so,
I'd edge my way into her backyard
pretending to look for my dog.

I wanted to get a closer look
at the face of the old woman bent
inside the ring of junipers and their wind-
ruined spires. Wanted to hear
her singing in an accent that sounded
something like my own grandmother's. I wanted
to get a better look at her stirring
and staring into the large kettle,
a brown scarf tied at her neck,
and a dark dress down
to her heavy black shoes.
I especially wanted to see the mixture
that she poured with heavy mits
from the cauldron into shallow pans to harden.

The alley between Hilda's backyard and ours
was cracked dirt and stickers—
my feet remember it well.
Even now they want to sneak me back
to that passage, that potion,
the bottomless cauldron.

* like homesickness, but more

A Matter of Time

It's only a matter of time until Charlotte, in *Hush...Hush Sweet Charlotte,*
finds her lover's hand dismembered, his head decapitated
on the night they are to elope. This was the last movie shown
in the small town before the theater closed for good—
the small town we moved to after the divorce.

On the movie's poster, Charlotte's eyes were full of terror,
her mouth shocked into a scream.
This, and the older kids' talk of a head rolling down a staircase
cemented images of a movie I was too young to see.
After we moved to that town, with the defunct theater,

I had a nightmare. I cannot talk about it. Even now—
my voice was paralyzed, but I could think.
I couldn't rebuke that evil spirit aloud, so my inner voice
cried *in the name of Jesus,* as I was taught. *Get behind me.*
And it left. And I woke. Or was I already awake?

Many things haunted me then and still about those years.
The storms out the upstairs window of my room where we lived
at the edge of town. Where down the embankment
cottonwoods grew along the muddy creek, would reach
for the sky—a thousand fingers electrified, the dark birds startled.

I've counted the buzzards preening and wing-flapping,
circling the water tower there like the restless hands
of a clock—little hands that fly away during the day
and come back at night to settle. All the images stacking up
like minutes you can't unwind.

Mr. Tate

Outside my window, the constant crickets
and crazy lady Tate's mumblings from the porch

of the blue stucco house next door.
Once her husband knifed her breast—

we were dancing, my girlfriends in the garage
when we heard noise above the radio. We sneaked

to the alley to see her running zigzag up and down
under the stars, one hand to her heart, screaming curses,

screaming he'd cut her. Mr. Tate used to sit
on his stoop evenings in overalls, smoking cigarettes,

his eyes like bloodshot water.
I'd say *hi Mr. Tate,* without stepping into his yard.

Their boy, Leon, a few years ahead of us
wore jeans that dragged the dirt, laughed and reeked

of beer when we'd ride bareback
on a friend's pony in the tar and gravel street.

Accused by other boys of messing
with a pig at the Ag barn, Leon was taken away.

Old man Tate died.
And now Mrs. Tate carries on two or more sides

of a conversation while she sweeps that small stoop.
She works the straw broom as if trying

to remove the serrated leg of a June bug
lodged deep in the concrete.

There had been too many shadows,
we couldn't see the blood. We barely had breasts.

Scar

There are scars and the ache between ribs.
A hitch in my breath, even now.
The memory of white shorts snagged
by a rusted barb and a scar wide
from no stiches. A scar hidden under
loose clothing—white clothes. My inner
thigh snagged. It was unsafe to cross
into the pasture. Watch out for snakes,
Mother said. Watch out for the bull
with its heifers. Don't misstep. Don't twist
the wrong way. Don't swim downstream
from the dead cow. Watch what you say
to Mr. Will. Don't get caught by the creek
at storm time. Watch out. Those white shorts.

Sound of Laughter

—*Denver, 1965*

Out back, the chestnut horse points its ears forward.
In the apartment living room, the mother cups her cheek.
Her other hand covers her mouth.

What had sounded like laughter was not.
The sisters cling to each side of the mother's dress.
The father avoids his daughters' eyes.

For a moment, the horse out back stops grazing.
The outing to the mountains is ruined.
The mother goes to her room.

The father lets the front door slam.
His jeep rumbles to a start.
The older sister runs to the pasture out back.

The horse lifts its head.
The younger child rearranges her ceramic cats.
Her sister returns from the pasture.

The father returns home after dark.
The earth's still trembling.
The sisters stay up past bedtime

drinking warm cocoa from rinsed pop bottles.
The horse out back sleeps standing up.
Less than an hour west, the Continental Divide moves closer.

The Trestle East of Darrouzett

My sister would lead.
Every few ties she'd wait,
would look back. *Hurry, hurry.*
Neither knew the train's schedule,
had no plan. Would we run?
Hang from a tie 'til the force
of the rumble shook
our fingers loose? The question
of balance and the odds of a train,
equally scary. Now, the trestle's
gone. Struck by lightning
while we slept. I stand among
its fallen parts—charred bits
half buried in dust, and squint up
at the severed rails splayed
like rigor mortis against the sky.
The low whistle of wind—condolences.

Winter Lullaby

The toe of her black patent lifted off
and off the damper's soft squeak.
In three-quarter's time, my mother cradled the notes
that echoed in the low-crafted ceiling above me.
My eyes followed the legatos moving
to the patterns in the braided rug—
three counts out and three counts back,
and floating up into the hollows
that housed the hammers and felt.
Through the window a sunbeam crossed the floor,
and lighted the grain in the spinet's leg.
In the end, the fermata. Then the silence.
She held it in her fingers, gently curved,
like the lashes of a child fallen to sleep.

Behind the Elevator

For Jay

I'm here, my back against this signpost,
prairie sky-scraper, holding pattern
for amber grains.
I'm distracted by what is missing—
train cars that once arrived empty
and left full.

Now, all the eighteen-wheelers
on state highway Fifteen carry the grain
through town. A different vibe,
one too rooted in the now—
and making new ruts
in summer's soft asphalt.

After the trestle caught fire,
the railroad was deconstructed—
the metal taken up for recycling,
and if I'd been warned, if I'd been here,
I would've gently hauled some ties
back east to my garden.

I don't usually stay for long,
so many voices, and a childhood erasing.
It can be hard to be still in a place
you thought you'd been craving.
Remember needing to get home
to your mother? Always needing
to get back to something?

The ladder leads to the high windows, eyes
that look past the long-faded
white-washed shadow
in which my head still smokes cigarettes,
and where my mouth
learned to exhale ring after ring.

I've come here through the breezeway—
the elevator's curtain
that divides the town from the fields,
the sidewalk from the isolated,
the rooted from some kind of free—

a tunnel from now to then
and back. I sit on the concrete stoop
that only looks south. My eyes
panning how the train went west to east, like me,
the sky turning deep.

It'll soon be dark,
and I'll take these arms and legs
back to the sidewalk,
and finally to the city.
This elevator stands over me, still
—*put out that cigarette*, it says. *Get on home.*

Silver Maple

You've been felled and lie scattered,
skewed in the green afterglow of an early evening rain.
Droplets fall from your morning whiskers.
Rain soaks your sides.
Quiet giant, you've been slain for being awkward,
messy, a hindrance.
Strange to see you sprawled along the ground,
your extremities and thick segmented torso
lodged in jumbled subjection.
The children run out with their imaginations on,
never knew they could climb so high.
In the morning when the sky is empty the chipper
will come and leave your ashes spread
under the Japanese saplings—such pretty little trees.

Prayer in the Bedroom Doorway

"It was never simple, even for birds, this business of nests"
Linda Pastan

Close your eyes and rest now. You have dressed them
to go out into the snow—coerced arms through sleeves,
forced feet into boots. How you lifted them,
and lifted them. Fed, bathed, woke them, took them to lessons
and buttered toast in your sleep.
You felt you'd be changing diapers forever—it wasn't so fleeting
at the time. So much is hidden now like the pony stencils
beneath two layers of paint, and the obvious absence embodied
in a well-made bed. Do not lament unremembered details.
You mustn't overthink trains with faces, princess quilts
and each thread you gave away or turned into rags.
May the hour be blessed now like then. Bedtime and waking
be blessed and dawn's calm on the face of every sleeping child
fortunate enough or not to hear *Winnie the Pooh* and *Goodnight Moon*—
Be grateful for the second-hand piano, and for hearing the youngest say
she couldn't sleep without an older one practicing down the hall.
Be grateful for duets and for the circle of fifths.
In the threshold of this milky light, close your eyes and listen.
In the still-strange quiet be grateful for fur, scales and wings.
Go now. Fling open the back door. Let the old dog charge
out into the yard with her ferocious bark.

Beacons

For Rhonda and Terry

Up here, in the north end of the town's cemetery
a concrete cross looks over the surnames and nicknames.

Over near the entrance is the town's new water tower—
a whitewashed block of a tank, bright as the cross

and placed on this high ground for gravity's sake,
for the sake of taking water to the living down highway Fifteen.

Even by night, the new tower is a stark blemish
amidst the hall of Junipers, the backdrop of graves and prairie.

Half a mile away, just off Main, is the old water tower.
As kids we'd climb it for kicks.

Its skinny legs are tarnished, the town's name is peeling,
but it still stands, a watchful eye.

At dusk, from May until winter, the buzzards cling to its rails.
From below it looks like a short black tattered skirt.

At dawn the birds lift off, and off, leave their excrement,
fly to the creeks, hide in the cottonwoods.

But how solid and clean the cross at the north end
of the cemetery stands, guarding its lambs and roses.

From miles it beckons.
We've sat here in its shadow, poured wine at its foot.

At Thirteen

"I've never been to heaven, but I've been to Oklahoma"
Three Dog Night, 1971

Chuck Taylor sneakers on the gym's wooden floor,
and *Three Dog Night* playing in the lounge
of the Student Center where I'd wait for Mom
(back to college after the divorce).
Beyond the brick of Business, Chemistry and Math,
it was just a small town. Dusty like all the rest—
a grain elevator at its edge next to the tracks,
and the train cars waiting there to be filled.

That summer? Wind, hot in my face.
Bobbie and I'd pull back the tarps truck after truck
pulled to a stop on the Co-op scale. The bushels of grain
would glint in the sun. We'd learn the names of the drivers
who'd soon follow summer to Kansas, Nebraska, then Iowa—
everything off to a different world—
the wheat into pits then poured into box cars headed east,
crews and combines to the north, and me headed to junior high

come late August where in science we'd stuff birds.
David killed one for me—I couldn't do it myself,
a pigeon, perched on the Co-op's windy eves come Fall.
All the birds in that town! Buzzards lining the water tower at dusk,
barn swallows in the corners of the front porch—
baby beaks chirping out from their cup-like nests, starlings
swooping, changing directions all at once against the pale sky.

For some time after, I thought of a boy named Kyle, a driver
out of west Texas. His truck, the maroon one.
I held to its side riding it from the scale to the dump pit
and back every time he came in from the field to weigh
and empty the grain.

That summer echoes mostly of a desire to hoist myself up
into the cabin of that truck. To ride as a passenger, that's all,

not as a way out—my mesmerized self not knowing what I didn't know.
I'd hoped he'd come back the next summer.
Maybe he's sitting mornings in a small town café
somewhere up in Iowa, telling stories of what it was like
to find that over each hill another wheat field was gold.

Burden

You held me on your lap
when what I wanted was to go outside to play.
I still hear your words in my head.

At your funeral, we said how you'd loved us.
Judging from all you gave us,
you did.

You visited me in college, took me to IHOP,
ordered crepes with lingonberries,
tipped the waiter, thanked the cook.

You used to say you carried a burden,
would talk for an hour
about the Apostle Paul. You'd ask

which side of the God fence I was on.
Would say I was starting to bloom.
The mink I never wanted

still hangs in my closet—
it wants to tell stories to the other coats
but it has no mouth.

Congregation

At ninety-four, you die in your own bed,
family surrounding you. My mother heard
that before your last breath you thrust your arms up,
palms open, as if reaching for God's embrace,
His promise to wrench the thorn,
the wound, the whole flesh—discard the earthly tent,
put the everlasting on.

*

My mother, sister and I take a seat behind the family.
One grandson sings, "Going Home."
Another reads the eulogy.
The congregation takes to the podium one by one telling stories—
how you helped pay the rent,
pay college,
buy glasses for a child, a car for a sister.
I sob.
People wail.
A woman lifts her hands, speaks in tongues.
It is not interpreted.

Listen

Out our bedroom window two men rebuild our chimney—
chisel away the cracked clay flue, the brick and mortar.
To drown the racket, I turn on *forest rain white noise.*
From a small speaker, I hear the pitter-patter,
an intermittent roll of thunder and distant bird calls.
Whatever thought I was having is interrupted by a memory
of the storm that moved in on us as we crouched, hushed,
on a river bank waiting to view the Macaws on the clay licks.
And that memory gives way to another—
takes me to the time when the weather had parted the skies
on a trip out west with the children—the violent rain
turning the caliche road slippery as ice.
The sound of rain takes me even further back to the clapping
and the torrential downpour outside a cheap room
in Miami Beach when you were just my boyfriend.

What did I come here to do today?

To listen to one sound drown another out?

The hammers and chisels lie still.
The two men sit in the grass, eating lunches
from paper bags. The older one speaks to the younger
in a language, that if only I could hear, I'd like to understand.

Emperor Penguins

How do they hear the other's voice
through all that chatter—thousands of callings, calling.

When I watch the footage they all look the same—
black and white with yellow-trimmed necks.

Patterns within patterns crowding across the frozen sea,
upright and formal in Antarctica's frigid air,

geography and primal instincts mandating the distance
one travels on feathered legs

from the breeding ground into the deep water
to forage for a next meal

that might keep the species alive.
Imagine knowing a voice—that voice,

and trekking starving miles over cliffs of ice
as if someone's life depends on it.

Leo Ferrari, 1927 - 2010

"My greatest fear is that some morning I'll wake up stark, raving sane."

You claimed to have nearly fallen off the edge
of the earth at Brimstone Head on Fogo Island.
The stories of you drew me in
not because *St. Augustine's Confessions*
was your favorite book, but because your other favorite
was Milne's, *Winnie the Pooh.* I never questioned
the curvature of the earth—my point of view
being that of grade school texts and photos from NASA.
You, on the other hand, maintained that the world is flat,
or possibly square, claiming that "a man
should always question the strongest convictions of his age,
for those convictions are invariably too strong."
I never heard you laugh, but those who did
say it was Dionysian. You, a professor at Halifax,
then St. Thomas, and Chatham, moonlighting
in summers as a butler to a multimillionaire at Pugwash.
Oh, to live that large—in awe of Antarctica's icy edge,
questioning gravity and outer space,
and gradually coming to realize, you once said,
"that science is only one of the many windows
through which we can look at the universe,
and a very small, murky window at that."

On An Early Sketch of Edward Hopper's, Seven A.M. 1948

If I could be in that upstairs window
behind the curved stroke

of your eye, what would I see? Myself,
looking back?

A teacher once said point of view is everything.
You, eternally unfinished,

were never-the-less spared
of the dark woods, the burdened strokes

that Hopper's loose copse of trees
became. It could have been you—

your hair grown so thick
and tangled across your aged lonely face.

You were spared, too, from that ambiguous
blue patch of sky—a constant question of weather.

From across the street where you once looked out,
and from where I looked back at you,

the morning sun inhabits a stark aqua wall,
and casts an angular shadow.

And you—his ghost covered, erased
or drawn back into that shadow.

.

Vester Kerns, Rexall Druggist

The sleeve and body of his lab coat
catch the camera's flash and brightly bleed
into the white edge.
It's little more than a glance of my grandfather's face,
the size of a quarter,
the cost of a shot at the local bar in those days.
He's looking down,
his eyes behind thin-rimmed glasses,
at the liquid inside the tube.
His coat, open at the top
exposes the knot of his tie.
What time of day was it at the Rexall?
Not that it would've mattered.
One week he'd bring home his pay,
and the next he'd be gone.
There's no date on this image,
but my grandfather's hair, combed back,
is lighter at the temple.
I'm told that some days he was kind,
and funny. He could make my grandmother laugh.
In this last photograph he holds a glass tube.
He holds his palms so close together
it looks almost like a prayer.

The Falls

for Slumber Valley Friends

From the first open wing of July the tiny daredevils
    flutter in spotlights of sun.

Their dusted wings barely missing
        the ripples in Meshoppen creek.

From cocoon to the last closed wing
    the white lichen moths dart in

and out of bluestone ledges way below the hardwoods
      that give the conifers life.

Until that last closed wing of October
    they gather in clusters above the ridges

where the creek pours over the edge.
      In summers we'd jump over

and over into holes formed in the flat rock below
    and pop up eye-level to the slippery moss,

a little less startled by the cold each time.
      Then we'd lie upon the ancient rock,

the heat from above and beneath, our swaddle.
    The sound of the falls, our silk.

Slipknot

All rote the way she guided the yarn
in her fingers to form an X, wove
the needle through, pulling the ends
to make a knot. Took the second needle
and adjusted for tension. My grandma
was always adjusting—moving from town
to town, four children and factory work
while my grandpa lost job after job.
He once begged her to lock him in a room.
His body shook and he cried until
the demons hid. He'd binge for weeks.
After he died, she moved close by.
My blue heaven, she called her rental.
Sports and game shows on TV,
her fingers stitching perfect rows
until at ninety-six they rested.
I take the last slippers she made,
pull the purls and the pink knots loose,
wind the string back into the skein,
back to when we shopped the end caps,
back to when I learned a slip-knot,
how to weave through and pull tight.
Then cast on, cast off, like she taught me.

White Sand

They wheeled my father back to wash him—
all the layers, with their trained hands.

They scrubbed off the elderly years of sponge baths,
and all those middle years of the occasional black bucket shower.

They scrubbed away the once-a-week bath of his boyhood
until he emerged with skin of a newborn

from the bath of his mother's womb. They patted him dry.
They swaddled him in sheets. Eden's sheets, yet unsoiled—

his body as weightless as before all
of the rest of his days began.

The dutiful hands had scrubbed
until the New Mexico sun disappeared like topsoil in wind.

They'd rubbed, turned and wrapped his skeleton body
in sheets of white sand. All but his head, they'd covered.

Three Kitchens

My father was leery of any food product with a long shelf life,
didn't approve of homogenized milk and insisted my mother
buy crunchy peanut butter, the kind that had to be stirred.
Our first kitchen had a window that looked out across the ditch
to where two horses grazed. He cooked food and ate meat back then.

The second kitchen—high in the mountains in an A-frame
built by my father—was so small my mother could reach
everything at once, but could not reach the things she needed.
We ate simple suppers on the braided rug, bathed in a sunken tub,
counted toilet paper squares.

We shared a third kitchen with my grandmother. Yellow café curtains.
I remember the black coffee aroma, and the lard next to the stove.
In Grandmother's house, my mother would stir chocolate on the burner,
then drop a spoonful into a bowl of cold water until it would take form.
She'd spread the fudge and pour into the pan to harden.

A breatharian believes he can live on air. I wanted to be convinced
that somehow it made sense, eating air. When my father died,
we found empty jars of Welch's grape juice under the kitchen sink
of his one-room apartment. My sister and I talked of keeping the jars.
Sometimes you have to say no. No, that isn't true.

City of the Sun: August

Already I need some shade
as we begin the tour around my father's three domes.
The sky's his fourth dome, his own heat lamp,
and occasional black bucket shower.
A bone-dry arroyo splits the earth nearby. The border,
a mile south, and the *Tres Hermanas* to the north
are equidistant. "Could walk there on a cooler day," he says,

and explains the past fifteen years: mixing concrete,
molding panels, raising and fitting them together,
packing the arcs in newspaper and red mud.
I see some is cracking, falling away.
"A full time job to stay ahead," my father says.

We walk around dome one to an east-facing
stained-glass window. *Beautiful*, I think.
"We humans were meant to wake," he continues,
"and go down with the sun, nap when it's hot."
I lean down and in: a mat of bright-woven blankets,
a plaid shirt old as me, a tan vest, jeans, all folded in squares.

Then, sky-lighted dome two for wheat grass.
Little clumps every few feet in various stages of growth.

Dome three for storage—an LL Bean fold-up bike,
handsaw, spools of twine, more newspaper, atlases.
Old bundled letters. I ask to look as I lower myself
to the concrete and leaf through a pile where I find,
in my younger handwriting, *Daddy, I hope you like it there.*
Can you hear coyotes?

"Forty or so dwellings," my father, in khaki shorts
and shirtless, says. His tanned hands gesturing out
to exoskeletons made of tires, bottles, and rusted busses.

Clumps of creosote bushes surround the domes.
If it rains they sprout flowers smaller than forsythia,

the color of aspen in fall, better seen up close to appreciate.
Father pinches off a few dark leaves, "chew them, they're medicinal."
I pick them from his palm, and place them on my tongue.
As he turns, I follow his bony back, and spit the bitters
onto the ground.

In Response to Kelly Schirmann's Poem, "[I feel too porous to read and too empty to write]" January 30, 2021 in *Poetry Daily*

Me too, Kelly—
feel too porous to read.
Like a sponge, wrung out and you say too empty to write.
You were still in bed.
I don't know what your bed looks like,
do not know the scent of your laundry detergent, or of you,
or even where you live.
But I hear you, fellow sea sponge.
My pillow is soft and I just want to go back under.

You get angry with yourself. *This is not how a poet is supposed to be.*
How is a poet expected to be? "It is in the green world,
among people, and animals, and trees," as Mary Oliver once said.
But where does the light go?
You say *the only way people can stand them* (poets)
is that we put our messes into a form.
What are we without the discipline of form?

I get you are *drained of your feelings just from being alive.*
I'm told this weariness too shall pass, and shall pass again and yet again
until I am diminished. Or maybe, made stronger?

I assume you want to remain a writer.
I was once walking an arroyo near Santa Fe and it came upon me.
It was, to me, God—the voice that gave me permission to be an artist.
I cried feeling that kind of love.
But today the smaller deities of lethargy, lack and indifference
are pecking away my vitality like crows.

I love buttered toast too.
You wrote, *when a tree is too slow to fruit, scientists invent new trees
with quicker apples.* I was affected. I hear you when you say
this thought makes me scared. But you caused me
to remember how good things come both quickly and slowly.
Like falling in love, and the fruits of commitment.

I applaud your poem. Bravo! It is a taste of hope.
The world is so fast for me.
But oh, that we may be
like a slow apple,
blossomed from a strong branch, skin expanding to protect the tart,
sweet, firm flesh. Each messy bite—may it nourish.

II.

Morning: Signs of the Human

Snow from last Thursday crouches in the shallow canyons
of these grasslands,
and drifts against the sixty miles of fence along the stretch
from Pampa to Perryton.
The snow nestles in the dry bed of Chicken creek,
and on the gray banks of the Canadian.
Nothing thaws for long until April comes around.
Signs of the human are scattered—
gas wells, windmills, cattle, power lines and this two-lane road.
The sky is colossal.
Here and there a scrub oak, bearing the wind.

Coal Creek Canyon

The cottonwood leaf in fall turns back to the color of aspen.

The boulders huddled here and there as if a giant hand
had nestled them where it wanted.
I'd scramble over the mossy shoulders and run
the needled ground back to the road lined with aspen—
their leaves flickering, like sun on moving water.
Each autumn the leaves dangled like gold coins without the weight.
The white gray bark was scratched in haphazard scars.
The marks, my father said, *show the age* of the slender trees.
My father built our A-frame so high up *you can see the Continental Divide.*
I'd stand on my tiptoes on the highest rock
and still I couldn't see. Suppers were quiet—
too quiet, too far, Mother said.
On a winter morning, we left—Mother, sister and me,
the switchbacks taking us down past the pines
that thin into junipers, into bare city trees. By late afternoon, just us
and the color of straw spread out both sides of the road.

The new creek is brown, stagnant except when it rains.
The cottonwoods lining the bank bend in one direction from the wind—
as determined to stay, it seems, as my mother was before she finally left.
One tree is uprooted and has fallen across the creek.
I sit on its coarse bark, dangling my feet over water that never does run clear.

Morning Passenger

*The gully brush, wheat fields and wooden fence posts measure
the distance to the homestead*

I scrape with my shoe some rough concrete
—a foundation claimed by crabgrass
and bitterweed, like a scab turned scar,
all that's left, this square, like the way a child
begins the drawing of a house,
complete with a hedge ripe with plums,
and stick cows over yonder.
From a prairie bird's eye we are but a glint,
some shapes and shades and shadows
in the early autumn sun.
Mother stays in the passenger's seat looking out
as if through a curtain so cottony thin
that a breeze could easily move it back
and forth across a rough wooden pane.

If I leave

I'll leave the sheers
that soften the bedroom
that has tried to be so good to me—
the small upper deck and out the window
the weeping cherry and river birches.
The shed of wreaths, strings of lights,
all partakers of the blooming
and falling, our first dog's gravestone:
You will stay with us. . .
That little dog lived for sixteen years—
one of the many numbers I use
to measure time. My youngest
was in her last year of high school
when the dog began to walk in circles.
I'd gone from accepting middle age
to being past. And my own parents
went from old to elderly. How pale
and shelled out my father's face.
                    But the sheers—I took them down once
to soak them in a tub. I rinsed
and fastened them to the clothesline.
Each soft pleat gestured fully in the wind.
When I brought them in,
and hung them back—so tame
on their rods—the scent of the outdoors
stayed for a time.
There's an airport on the edge of the city,
planes taking off, or about to land.
I sometimes watch them over the trees.
The air today, beneath a thousand wings,
is barely a draft under the curtain hem.
It's just enough to lift the cloth,
and settle it back down on the sill.

Peaches

Aunt Daisy in short heels, ample in her apron and pearls
set the dish down in front of me—
thick-sliced peaches
drenched in raw heavy cream—
a taste so luscious, I wanted to ask for more.
Downy, with a creamy-gold under color, sunrise
all around. When whole and ripe
the second bite's easier than the first.
And it goes from there—messy, juicy,
until all that's left is the rough-ribbed stone—the last bit,
like that longing of a moment fulfilled,
though only for that moment.
Aunt Daisy, with your *pearls of great price,*
and your apron stained with juice,
reach up again, your hand, into the branches.

• italics from R.S. Thomas' "Bright Field"

Ode to a Tractor

for Jenni and in memory of Lynn Roper

Old Green hasn't turned the soil in decades.
Put out to pasture, it sits at the south end
of a retired section near an empty schoolhouse—
its hood pointing east.
Nestled in prairie weeds, firewheels,
and primrose, its parts wear the cycles
of weather. Of the morning dew, afternoon heat,
and the stars that rise and cross the sky.
Field mice that once scurried from its pickers
now shelter in the walls of its dry-rotted tires.
I drove that tractor in my fifteenth summer,
green as a grasshopper. No cab, no umbrella.
Just a new radio with one decent station.

Like Nothing Before

Although his mother feeds him pancakes, makes him
two sandwiches to take to school for lunch, and after school,
makes him cinnamon toast with melted pats of butter,
and for supper all the meat he wants, still, the boy feels half full.

The boy wants the dog like nothing ever before.
The parents forbid it. The boy buys the old greyhound
with money he's saved, hides his dog in a bomb shelter,
feeds him in secret. Then the boy falls ill.

In post WWII Britain, parents aren't allowed to visit their child
in the hospital more than three times in a week.
The boy is alone. The dog is hungry. The boy worries.
The dog does not understand. But everyone is well

by the time this story ends. When I was thirteen, I fell in love
with my sister's boyfriend. He moved. My sister stopped writing to him.
I used to write to him. He'd write me back, asking about my sister.
Harsh realities are not entirely redeemed by okay endings.

But the tastes of Sundays at my grandmother's, swimming
in deep clear water, a lover when love begins—these
have made me feel full. It's been decades
and I have not forgot the first story that ever made me cry.

Mercy Rain

for Bobbie

Your mama died—a clot—before your third grade summer.
The town had poured into the auditorium.
Some time later, a familiar kind of rain began, hard and stuttered—
cool drops in exchange for weeks of heat. Then a downpour
that washed the melon from our chins.
We'd carried it from my mother's kitchen to the road.
With its slippery weight above our heads,
we smashed it onto the pavement of Plummer.
In the middle of the rain we scooped the jagged pieces up,
and tore at the flesh with our permanent teeth.
With our whole faces we ate to the rinds, throwing them up
into the small elms, chasing barefoot— hooting, hollering, loosed
and spitting seeds until we lay along the curb—the rainwater
like a warm creek running over and beside us
and through our long hair—a rain that had begun in hesitant drops
now lifting the low incense of tar and gravel from the street.

Matriarch

In the riverbed, an echo of pounding,
a pulse, a solace gathered in the silt.

"The cloud is an elephant," she says,
as we fly from her home to mine.

I look out to see a trunk siphoning water,
the outline of an ear, and one small eye

gazing past another cloud.
The rest dissipates into cirrus.

We once watched elephants in east Africa.
We learned how they nuzzle the bones of their dead,

feel the dried skulls with the soles of their feet,
pass their mourning and their memory

on to the next generation.
I study my mother's face as she rests now,

and close my eyes as well. Against my own dark lids,
I see the matriarch.

I hear the trumpet as she celebrates birth.
Elephant families gather at the river to drink,

and they play, even the old,
when they feel safe.

Church Nursery

Did the sound of my own crying, crying myself to sleep,
create the phonological loop
that allowed for this earliest memory?

Waking, looking around,
looking for my mother through the slats
from inside a crib whose sheets weren't mine.
Strangers rocking, pale walls,
incandescent light, a hubbub of voices.

Disoriented upon waking someplace unfamiliar—
it happens still.
Relieved when the familiar walks in.

Studies suggest that when a past event is remembered,
the brain reconstructs that event in reverse order.
I swim down to where deep water ponies
parade across nursery walls.

My mother came back.
I can feel the fabric of her dress—
my neurons responding still
to the somatosensory cortex,
to the tactile stimuli of feel, and touch,
to that encoding—the separation
of my clenched hands from the fabric of her dress.

Beneath the Pines

for Kristy

I'd brush away the needles, push and twist that spoon
into the black-gold dirt—you'd do the same—
until it'd scrape something hard,
then wedge the spoon, pry out the rock, blow it off—
tiny points of grays, purples, and yellows like yellowed glass.
We'd lick our shirts, shine the stones until they glittered,
then dig for another.

When I moved, we wrote for a time.
I remember the loops of your young cursive, feel even now
as if I could trace your name,
still feel the days when calcite crystals were diamonds,
when tobacco-colored needles filled my eyes.
I want to still wear that awe of wonder on my face,
and feel the drive of that dig in my hands.

Jan Taggert

We raced and you won. That's why I remember your name.

Heat rising, mirage on the junior high track, lanes marked.

One hundred meters.
            Was I not quick enough off the block?
Did I run zigzag, losing that fraction of a second?

I awake. The sky has lifted the dew
from a pristine parking lot where I'm teaching my child
to pedal her bike. I hold on and let go. Hold, let go.
My daughter circles the lot until she and her bike are dizzy.

When I awake, you are still with me, Jan—
Jan, with the short sandy hair, sturdy build
and blue framed glasses strapped around your head.

The starter's pistol snaps.
In my periphery—your shoulder, your neck stretching out
milliseconds past mine.

This first loss was when I had nothing
to blame but my own body—

                one hundred meters.
No sky, no field.
You, in the next lane.

And when I awake, you are still with me.

Polio Summer

after John David Lundberg

We played army, picked haw haws, and once I got stuck
in the thick tree in Ella's yard.
We'd take turns winning King of Lister Hill,
would fly kites there, and slide
over the grass on cardboard.
Many things preceded the infection,
preceded that day when me and my brother, Lee,
went swimming in the fountain at Parade Park.

My feet used to pound the sidewalk
down Lister Hill, so steep that when I began to run,
I was nearly falling. This is my most vivid memory
of self-locomotion, what it was to walk and run.
It was in a childhood blink—that bumpy moment
of the gurney's approach to the hospital ER.
All the things I looked at one way,
I'd look back on another.

Though I remember venetian blinds raised
and lowered, holidays surrounded by white,
and playing with toy soldiers my parents brought,
I can't remember that big event
of leaving the hospital—in an ambulance Lee says—
after eleven months.

Earlier that summer, Lee had taken me to see
The Shadow at the theater on Belmont about a guy
trapped in a place and the walls moving in.
That summer, before it happened, we'd sit evenings
on the porch and play "go to the head of the class."
Everyone started on the bottom step
and moved up by correctly guessing
which hand held the rock.

The Dawning

From the doorway of a convenience store
just off a mid-summer, mid-west exit,
he stretches halfway under our truck—
the body flush against days of oil and dust
washed and unwashed away. He scans
the underside, finds the leak that trickles
from beneath the axle and metal that shelter
our children who stir inside in stages
of dreams, wakefulness, and three days
of travel to go.
                    The sun frees the dew from the pumps
and asphalt of the world, reopens my eyes
to one who rises from the shadow
and who, in the early light, is unveiled
as it was in the garden before the tempting.
Before all the rest of our days began.
I stand in the clearing of that first morning,
tomorrow's weight like a stone rolling away.
I want to go to him—to light on his shoulder,
tell him all the goodness I remember.

The Sand Hills

for Ruth

There was always sand, but time had you wait
for the wet salty air off the Eastern shore,
and for the opaque waves breaking on the rough gem

of the Cape's jetty. It had you wait for someday
when the sun would lift bits of sea from your skin,
when the dune grass would cut at your shins,

and the sound of a seagull, diving for a scrap,
would enter your ear until at last, you'd hardly notice.
Evening after evening now you spot from the shore

whole families of dolphins as they rise
and dip before the waters thicken, before it all blends
with the color of dusk.

You can name the birds—the Sanderling
and the Willet. Maybe you can still hear the screech
of a prairie hawk above an open sky

or see the buzzards that perched on the water tower
each evening. When you were small
you'd hunt for the endangered horned toads

in the parched grass. When lucky enough to catch one,
you'd turn it over, stroke its belly—rounded and rough
like a dry tongue— and let it go.

Remember what it was to roll down the Sand Hills
over and over, far from any body of water, eyes tight shut,
the hot grains needling into your skin? At the base

of one of those hills was a red pump. You'd put your face,
mouth wide open, under its spigot. As if it could quench
your thirst, the cold water would burst forth in gulps.

Saluté

Tanqueray and tonics, extra lime for both
in a small cove in the old port of Palermo at a table
made from a barrel. Behind us, the narrow streets
and graffitied walls. Beyond, the sailboats rest,
rows upon rows upon rows of masts.

Close by, a bride and her groom,
followed by a photographer, sweep along a pier.
The train of her dress graces each plank,
out into the harbor out into the sea. He dips her backward,
her laughing, his hand at the small of her back.

Watching, we lift our glasses, *Saluté*,
in their direction as the water laps the shore barely,
and the sun now barely lights the sky.
The waiter lights the candle on our table.

Before we finish our next drink I say
"Remember after college, Miami Beach? Before
you flew to New York and I left for Texas,
the highway motel, the thunder and hard rain?"
                                What makes a long marriage,
a long marriage?

Down by the water, a stone wall crumbles
and a skinny kitten chases a scrap of paper.
All lines go soft in the yellow light.

Short Affair

Steven Zear was my love. He promised *forever,*
gave me a locket engraved with a Z.
But somehow in the mess of kindergarten and family
and fall affairs, his mother found her locket missing.
Had Steven confessed?
It's vague now— his mother walking out of their brick home.
My mother handing her the locket and chain
through the car window, some mumblings, a chuckle.

There would be more car windows and the taking of gifts
from a man who did not seem to know what was
and wasn't his to give— school clothes, a fur coat.
The first time I took candy from Mr. Will's extended hand,
what was I supposed to learn? The exhilaration
of running all the way home, heart beating like a rabbit's?

And what about Steven's heart, in his little chest that day?

1959 D-Mule Penny

On its obverse side, the head of Lincoln. On the reverse,
     the obsolete wheat design instead of the new memorial.
The experts call this mix the *mule penny,*
     different back and front than it should be. A mismatch.
Error, or better, mischief of the coin artists.

     The penny passes through twenty-seven years
of unknowing fingers before a collector discovers it,
     and even with its authenticity in question,
the hybrid cent sells for $48,000 at an auction in 2003.

     Take the mule itself—mix of a mare and donkey,
more valuable than the chariot horse,
     favored by the Kings of Israel, known in Egypt
before the time of Moses.
     Not only do they eat less than horses and are hardier,
as George Washington discovered,
     but they live longer so he bred them, they multiplied
and by the time Lincoln came along,
     the states had thousands. Not so with the rare mule coin.

In 1959, a gallon of gas is twenty cents,
     the U.S. children hear names like *Vietnam,*
Alaska is newly admitted as the 49th state.
     My sister is two. My parents are unhappy together.
My grandmother reunites with her alcoholic husband
     in Fairbanks, Alaska, city of the northern lights.

All her life, my mother is repulsed by the smell of whiskey—
     As a teen, she joins the Nazarene church,
learns it's wrong to wear lipstick and jewelry,
     feels she's dangling over the pit of hell for wanting.
Maybe that's one reason my agnostic father, minimalist that he is,
     falls in love with her.

In 1963 my grandfather moves from the northern lights
     to Texas, to his early sober death. Mother tells the kind version

of his life—smart chemist, walked on his hands,
        always had a joke. She says a person shouldn't expose
a man's nakedness, which is biblical, but I go back and forth,
        heads or tails, things hidden in plain sight.

Paddling Together

—thirty four years

On a different day the rain clouds might darken the sky
—bright buoyant breezes turning to gusts,

the boat's waterline keeping time with the waves,
our foreheads lined with worry.

But today, in the middle, we smile at how still it is.
A fish jumps. Maybe a bass? After a time, we paddle the canoe

beneath a mix of hardwoods, scraggly pines,
and underbrush. Here, the water's shallow

—roots, strings of moss, small stones,
and the silt that lifts like minor dust clouds.

I slap at a mosquito. This lake was once a river.
How wide and deep and fast did it run?

Oblong rocks, smoothed over by time
must be settled in the middle, in the dark cold calm.

I wonder how many days-turned-years it took
to fill the bowl under the body of this boat,

to what determined edge. We push off again,
find our stride, follow the invisible wake.

April Snow

Was late afternoon—fingers stretched from two horizons
forming duck feet webs of gray-white

until all the sky was just that—when from nowhere
a Great Blue Heron landed at the pond and snatched our last koi.

Afterward, I drove to the store for plastic Easter eggs
and chocolate. Just past dusk, with snow ankle deep, I traipsed

back through the parking lot, inching home, the onion flakes
falling on the windshield like cherry blossoms,

and the wipers whisking them away as fast as they landed—
a motion that jolted my thoughts back to the earlier event

at the pond— the speed of the heron, its muscled legs,
blue-green. Its great wings landing and lifting off,

and Albert's orange iridescence wriggling in the spear-like bill.
I had run after it, waving both arms to the sky, shouting

let him go, let him go! And like that, the bird dropped the fish
on the driveway— the terrible flapping —just to scoop it back up.

There's an absence when you climb the snowy steps,
dark past dusk, next to a newly fishless pond.

An emptiness different than silence.
One that is distinct from the quiet you hear

when you know a loved one is just in the next room
reading or having a cup of tea.

After

for Goodguy

He pushes out of the chair
and begins walking,
wearing his old fedora
and his generous wool coat.

He finds a bench by a pond,
a green pond,
and sits watching
the rings in rings
in rings of rain.

In this band of light—
this circle
of once more
once—I go
to sit beside him,
to be covered by his coat.

Evening Church

The song leader lifts his wings,
let the birds fly across the earth, the expanse of the heavens.
And my mother does. She flies up into the rafters,
full-throated *Rock of Ages*. Around the little suns
she soars in chorus with doves and mockingbirds,
the beams of evening's stained glass filling her lungs
with crimson and gold.

I'm down below on the pew, a little egg
not yet hatched, waiting for her to come back and warm me.
I know what it is to be covered by a wing
and have the feathers lift off and off
until the singing finally stops.

The congregants turn wispy pages to Psalm 42,
as the hart panteth after the water brooks,
so panteth my soul after Thee, O God,
and they wonder at what a deer panting by a stream
could mean, but accept it as a symbol of themselves.
At the suggestion of thirst, my mother
hops down and bounces under the benches—
quietly, as not to disturb—to the fountain
at the back of the sanctuary.

When I'm hatched and pushed off into my own classroom,
I continue to learn about thirst in string, felt
and pieces of straw, and learn the alphabet too.
But some days what I want is to be nested
between my mother's wing and the polished firmament,
to not even try in my small hollow bones
to figure out things I don't know, I don't know.

Claire McGoff is a poet, wife, mother and grandmother. Her work has appeared in *Image Magazine, Innisfree Poetry Journal, Beyond Words Literary Magazine*, and has been included in *Snowdrops*, a collection of winter poems by *Wingless Dreamer*. Claire enjoys participating in several writing circles, including a group of poets who have met bi-monthly for the past 15 years. She is a 2018 graduate of the Warren Wilson MFA Program for Writers.

Claire grew up in Colorado and in the Texas panhandle. After college, she moved to New York state where she completed an internship in Dietetics while getting married and starting a family. After several years in New York, she and her husband settled in Maryland where they expanded their family and raised six children and many pets. During these years, Claire served in various volunteer positions in her children's school including the lunch program and hospitality.

In addition to poetry, Claire relishes her family, friends, traveling, live music and being in nature.

From These Outskirts is Claire's debut collection.

www.ingramcontent.com/pod-product-compliance
Lightning Source LLC
Chambersburg PA
CBHW021202090426
42740CB00008B/1198